D0971549

The BATHROOM FUNNY PAGES

———————•———————

Russ Edwards
Jack Kreismer

RED-LETTER PRESS, INC.
Saddle River, New Jersey

Red-Letter Press, Inc.
P.O. Box 393
Saddle River, NJ 07458
www.Red-LetterPress.com

ACKNOWLEDGEMENTS

EDITORIAL:
Jeff Kreismer & Kobus Reyneke

•

TYPOGRAPHY:
Christina Chybinski & Matt Taets

•

COVER:
Cliff Behum

The
BATHROOM
FUNNY PAGES

———————•———————

The Anniversary Joke

Ralph forgot his wedding anniversary and his wife was more than a bit agitated. "Tomorrow morning, I expect to find a gift in the driveway that goes from 0 to 200 in five seconds. And it better be there or else!" she yelled.

The next morning Ralph woke up early to do his thing. When his wife got up, she looked out the window and sure enough there was a gift-wrapped box, smack in the middle of the driveway. The wife put on her robe and slippers, ran outside and opened it up right then and there – a bathroom scale.

———— • ————

**If you want to read about love and marriage
you've got to buy separate books.**

—Alan King

• • •

The Air Force Joke

Twin brothers are hoping to enlist in the U.S. Air Force. The recruiting officer says to the first twin, "Any skills of a military nature?" "I'm a pilot," he replies.

The recruiter knew he had struck gold. He stood up and shook the man's hand. "Welcome to the Air Force ... And what about you?" the officer asks the second twin. "I chop wood."

"Sorry. We really don't need any wood choppers," says the officer. "But you enlisted my brother." "Yeah, well he's a pilot," says the officer.

The twin shakes his head, rolls his eyes and responds, "Maybe so, but I have to chop the wood before he can pile it!"

· · ·

The Antique Joke

A savvy antiques collector was walking through an artsy section of San Francisco when he noticed a mangy old cat lapping milk from a saucer in the doorway of a ceramic shop. He recognized instantly that the saucer was a long sought piece missing from the estate of George Washington and a veritable national treasure, so he entered the store and slyly offered to buy the cat for ten dollars.

The owner said, "Sorry, it's not for sale."

"Please, I have an awful problem with mice around my house. I could use the old tomcat to catch them. I'll tell you what. I'll double my offer for him."

The owner shot back, "Twenty dollars it is. He's all yours."

The collector picked up the cat and said, "I wonder if you'll throw in that old saucer with it. I noticed the cat drinking out of it and it'll save me from having to buy another dish."

"Nothing doing buddy," the owner replied. "That's my lucky saucer. So far I've sold 62 cats."

The Army Joke

"I suppose once you get discharged from the Army, you'll barely be able to wait until I die so you can spit on my grave," growled the drill sergeant.

"Not me," responded the private. "Once I'm out of the Army, I'm never gonna stand in line again!"

• • •

The Auction Joke

The bidding was fast and furious at a local auction when, at one point, the auctioneer received a note to read aloud. "A gentleman at today's auction has lost his wallet which contains $10,000. He has offered a $1,000 reward for its return."

From the back of the room, a voiced boomed out, "One thousand, five hundred!"

THOUGHTS OF THE THRONE

"I grew up with six brothers. That's how I learned to dance – waiting for the bathroom."
—Bob Hope

The Bar Joke

A bartender walked over to a guy with a frog on his head and said, "Hey, where'd you get that?"

"Believe it or not," the frog croaked, "it started out as a wart on my butt."

•

A guy sporting a snoot full leaves a bar, waves down a taxi and says to the cabbie, "Take me to the corner of 45th and 5th."

"This is the corner of 45th and 5th," responds the cabbie.

"Thanks," the drunk belched, "but next time don't drive so fast."

•

A hotel desk clerk gets a call at four in the morning.

"Shay, can you tell me what time the bar opens?" asks a rather sloshed fellow.

"11 A.M."

A bit later, the clerk gets another call from the same guy, who's now even more plastered. He slurs, "What time doesh the bar open?"

"Same time as I told you before, sir – 11 A.M."

An hour passes by and the clerk receives one more call from the drunk who is definitely three sheets to the wind. "Shay, what time-jushay shat shuy bar openshup?"

"11 A.M., sir. But if you want, you can order in and we'll send up room service."

"Lissten Buddy, I don' wanna ged in, I wanna ged out."

Two guys are sitting at a bar and become quite tipsy. The first guy says, "Say, where are you from?"

The second fellow says, "I'm from Miami."

The first guy replies, "Really? I'm from Miami, too. What high school did you go to?"

The second guy answers, "St. Joe's."

"Incredible!" remarks the first guy. "Me, too!"

"Wow!" says the second guy. "What year did you graduate?"

"'83."

"My gosh. I graduated in '83, too!"

"Looks like we're in for a long one tonight," the bartender sighs to one of the other customers. "The O'Malley twins are drunk again."

•

A bartender says to the customer, "What'll it be?"

"I'll have a martinus."

"You mean a martini, right?"

"If I wanted two of 'em, I'd order two of 'em."

•

A guy stepped up to the bar and ordered a martini. Before drinking it, he delicately removed the olive from the glass and put it into a small jar he took from his pocket. After downing the drink, he ordered another and again took the olive from it and placed it into the jar. He repeated this process several times until the jar was full of olives. He then paid the bar tab and staggered out. A customer who saw what had gone on said to the bartender, "Boy, that was really weird."

The bartender answered, "What's so odd about that? His wife sent him out for a jar of olives."

•

Steinmetz was sentenced to 20 years of solitary confinement. Bored to death after about two years of his jail stay, he spotted an ant crawling across the floor of his cell. Then he got a brainstorm. "Hey, I've got plenty of time to kill ... I'll train this ant to do tricks."

Train him he did, first to do really simple things, then to do flips and somersaults. Steinmetz eventually taught the ant to juggle, to sing and even to do impressions of George Clooney, Bill Clinton, Sanjaya Malakar and the like. He even worked up a comedy routine as Hot Snoop Diggety Dog, a hip-hop artist who only raps Perry Como songs. The bug was, in a word, boffo.

When Steinmetz's sentence was finally over, he left the prison with the ant and the knowledge that he had a surefire show biz act. But before seeking out an agent, the man decided to celebrate his freedom with a drink. He went into a tavern, sat down and placed the ant on the bar in front of him. As the bartender approached, Steinmetz said, "See this ant?"

"Sure do," the bartender exclaimed as he squashed the ant under his thumb. "Now what's your pleasure?"

A middle-aged fellow stops into a bar for a nightcap. He strikes up a conversation with the bartender and says, "I just went to my first night school class."

"Really... what'd you learn?" asks the bartender.

"I learned to write."

"Hey, on your first day? That's terrific! What did you write?"

"Dunno...I can't read."

•

A guy walks into a bar and orders two martinis. The bartender serves them and says, "If it's all the same to you, pal, I could have made a double and used one glass."

The guy says, "Oh, I know, but my best buddy died and, just before he did, I promised him I'd order him a drink every time I came in here."

The next week the guy comes back and says to the bartender, "I'll have a martini."

The bartender says, "And one for your buddy, too?"

He says, "Oh, no. This is for my buddy. I'm on the wagon."

THOUGHTS OF THE THRONE

"I hated having to wake up in the middle of the night to walk to my bathroom – where suddenly there was a six-foot-seven-inch, headless figure with a sword and a horse!"

—Johnny Depp

A cowboy moseyed out of the saloon to find that some scallywag had painted his horse yellow. He swaggered back through the swinging doors of the tavern and barked, "All right, which one of you no-good, low-down sidewinders painted my horse yellow?"

At the end of the bar, a huge hunk of a man stood up and roared, "I did ... and what are you gonna do about it?"

The cowboy responded in his most pleasant tone, "I just thought you might like to know that it's about ready for a second coat."

•

A seal walks into a tavern and the bartender says, "What'll you have?" "Anything but a Canadian Club."

•

A skeleton goes into a bar and says, "Give me a beer... and a mop."

•

A five-dollar bill walks into a saloon. The bartender says, "You'll have to leave. This is a singles' bar."

•

A priest, a minister and a rabbi walk into a bar and the owner goes up to them and says, "What is this? Some kind of joke?"

•

A brain walks into a bar and the bartender says, "Sorry, I can't serve you."

"Why not?" asks the brain.

"You're already out of your head."

A horse walks into a fun-loving drinking establishment and the bartender says, "Why the long face?"

•

A ham sandwich walks into a bar. The bartender says, "We don't serve ham sandwiches."

The sandwich says, "That's okay, I just want a beer."

•

An astronaut and his buddy bounce into a bar on the moon and the astronaut complains, "The drinks are okay, but there's no atmosphere."

•

Maybe you've heard of the not-too-bright would-be lawyer who walked into a bar and said, "So is this where I take the exam?"

•

A grasshopper goes into a saloon and hops up onto a seat at the bar. The bartender looks at the grasshopper and says, "Hey, we have a drink named after you."

The grasshopper says, "You have a drink named Harry?"

•

A guy walks into a bar with a slab of asphalt under his arm and says, "A beer please. Oh, and one for the road."

•

A golf club walks into a bar. The bartender says, "I can't serve you."

"Why not?" says the golf club.

"Because you'll be driving soon."

A penguin goes into a saloon and asks the bartender, "Have you seen my brother?"

"I don't know. What does he look like?"

•

A pair of jumper cables goes into a bar. The bartender says, "Alright, I'll serve you, but don't start anything."

•

A ghost walks into a tavern at closing time. The bartender says, "Sorry, we don't serve spirits at this time of night."

•

Did you hear about the dyslexic guy who walked into a bra?

•

A tipsy guy staggers up to a parking meter. He puts in a quarter, the needle stops at 60 and he exclaims, "I can't believe it – I lost 100 pounds!"

•

A pony goes into a bar and says, "How about a hot toddy? I'm a little hoarse."

•

A giraffe goes into a bar and the bartender says, "Do you want a longneck?"

•

A drunk walked into a bar. He needed five stitches.

•

A talking dog goes into a bar and says, "How about a drink for the talking dog?"

The bartender responds, "OK, the toilet's right around the corner."

Two tubs of yogurt go into a bar. The bartender says, "We don't serve your kind here."

One of the yogurt cans retorts, "Why not? We're cultured individuals."

———— • ————

**I went up to a girl in a bar once and asked her where she was from.
I guess she wasn't interested, because she said, "Mars."
So I asked, "You need a ride home?"**

—Ray Romano

• • •

The Barnyard Joke

Three pigs are in the barnyard. The first one says, "Oink, oink." The second pig says, "Oink, oink, oink."

The third pig says, "Moooo."

The other two pigs do a double take. Overhearing the third pig, the farmer asks, "What did you say?"

"Mooooooo."

"That's crazy," says the farmer. "Pigs don't say, 'moooo'!"

"I know," the third pig says. "But I'm trying to learn a second language."

The Baseball Joke

A slick-fielding baseball player was walking by a burning building. A mother with a baby in her arms yelled to him from the third floor. The ballplayer told her to drop the baby. She let go, he caught the baby, then whirled and threw it to first base.

•

A baseball player died and went to Heaven. Once up there, he was able to look down to Hell, where he saw the most spectacular stadium with a capacity crowd, players on the field and a batter at the plate.

"Boy, St. Peter," the ballplayer said. "It looks like a game is just about to start. You call that Hell? I'd love to be playing there."

"That's just it," smiled St. Peter. "So would they, but they don't have a ball."

• • •

The Bathroom Joke

There was a rootin-tootin cowboy who sashayed to the outhouse in back of the saloon. He heard a noise coming from inside, so he looked down the hole. Sure as shootin', there was an old Indian looking back up. The cowboy offered him a hand and said, "Poor fellah. How long have you been stuck down there in that awful hole?"

The Indian answered sadly, "Many moons."

———— • ————

Did you hear about Robin Hood's house?
It has a little John.

The Beethoven Joke

Beethoven's Ninth Symphony is being performed at the famed Carnegie Hall. During intermission, the conductor becomes frantic when he realizes the last few pages of his sheet music are missing. After telling his assistant this, the trusted aide remembers that the missing pages were accidentally locked in the dressing room. He assures the conductor that they'll be on his music stand in time for when they are needed.

"I would hope so," growls the conductor. "And while you're at it, keep an eye on the bass players. They've been drinking ever since the intermission started."

The conductor then goes about his business while the assistant makes sure the bass players down a few cups of coffee before they return to their orchestra seats. As the curtain rises for the remainder of the symphony, the assistant rushes to find a security guard who can open the dressing room. He finds one and hurries him down to the locked room.

"What's all the fuss about?" asks the security guard.

The assistant replies, "It's the bottom of the ninth, the score is tied, and the bassists are loaded!"

The Beggar Joke

Down in the canyons of Wall Street, a fabulously wealthy stockbroker passed a bedraggled beggar dressed in rags.

"Please, sir, may I trouble you for a dollar so that I might get a bite to eat?" pleaded the beggar.

"You poor fellow," said the stockbroker. "Come with me and I'll buy you a drink."

"Actually, sir, I don't drink, but I would like a bite to eat."

"Here, my good man. Take one of my special stock of Cuban cigars," urged the broker.

"Sorry, sir," said the bum. "I don't smoke."

"Then come with me down to Atlantic City. I'll stake you in the casino and you might win enough to get your life back on track."

"I can't do that, sir. I don't gamble, but I would still like a bite to eat."

"You want to eat?" asked the stockbroker. "Very well, come home with me and have dinner with us."

"That's very kind of you, sir. Thank you."

"Not at all," replied the broker. "I just want my wife to see what happens to a man who doesn't drink, smoke or gamble."

———— • ————

My family was so poor, they couldn't afford to have any kids.
The lady next door had me.
—Lee Trevino

The Blonde Joke

A man was mowing his front lawn when his gorgeous neighbor came out of her house and went straight to the mailbox. She opened it, slammed it shut and went back into the house.

A few moments later she came out again, went to the mailbox and repeated the action. She came out a third time, opened the mailbox and once again slammed it shut. Curious of her actions, the man asked, "Is something wrong?"

"There certainly is ... My stupid computer keeps saying, 'You've got mail!'"

•

Q: How come blonde jokes are so short?
A: So brunettes can remember them.

•

Paris Hilton goes into a department store and tells the salesman she's looking for a blue curtain. He shows her a wide selection of blue fabrics and then asks, "What size curtains do you need?"

She answers, "Just 19 inches."

Surprised, he says, "19 inches! What room are they for?"

She replies, "I only need one, and it's not for a room. It's for my computer monitor."

The intimidated salesman sputters, "But ma'am, computers do not have curtains."

To which Paris Hilton remarks to the clerk, "HELLOOooooo.... I've got Windows!"

Did you hear the one about the blonde who saw a sign in the ladies room that said "Employees Must Wash Hands"? She waited and waited all evening for one to come but finally had to do it herself.

——— • ———

**Assume nothing. Inside every dumb blonde
there may be a very smart brunette.**

—Ann Landers

——— • ———

**Barbie is getting a bigger waist and a smaller chest.
Not surprisingly, earlier today Ken announced
he wants to start seeing other dolls.**

—David Letterman

• • •

The Bungee Joke

Jeff and David dreamed of owning their own bungee jumping business. The trouble was that all the good spots were taken and getting a place in an amusement park in the states was just too expensive. Then, they hit upon an idea – Set up a bungee tower in Mexico where expenses would be lower.

They pooled their money and bought a tower, bungee cord, and all the other equipment they would need. As they assembled the tower in a small resort town, a group of locals gathered to watch. Finally, it was time to test the system.

After being selected as the guinea pig, the bungee cord was attached to David's feet, and over he went. When he bounced up again, he was bruised and scratched but Jeff couldn't quite catch him. The next time he bounced up, he was bleeding a bit and had a broken nose. Jeff still couldn't catch him. The third time he bounced, Jeff finally grabbed his battered body and pulled it over to the platform, where David collapsed in a heap.

"What happened?" Jeff asked with great concern. "Was the bungee cord too long?"

"No," David croaked. "But what the Hell is a piñata?"

• • •

The Camping Joke

Sherlock Holmes and Dr. Watson were on a camping trip deep in the English countryside. They had retired for the evening and were lying there, looking up at the sky. Holmes said, "Watson, look up. What do you see?"

"Well, I see thousands of stars."

"And what does that mean to you?" said Holmes.

"Well, I guess it means we will have another fine day for the great outdoors tomorrow. What does it mean to you, Mr. Holmes?"

"To me, my dear Watson, it means someone has stolen our tent!"

The Car Joke

Harriet's husband Herb, an inveterate automobile enthusiast, died suddenly one day. When she went to take care of the funeral arrangements, the local undertaker asked her how she wanted the obituary to read. Harriet asked, "What's the cost?"

"A dollar per word," replied the undertaker.

"Okay," Harriet said. "I want it to read 'Herb is Dead'."

The undertaker responded, "I'm sorry. It's a six word minimum."

Harriet thought for a second and then said, "Okay, 'Herb is Dead, Corvette for Sale'."

———— • ————

I had to stop driving my car for a while. The tires got dizzy.
—Steven Wright

• • •

The Caterpillar Joke

Two caterpillars are strolling along in the park when one sees a butterfly go by, points up at it and says to the other, "You'll never get me up in one of those things."

The Centipede Joke

The turtles and skunks decide to have a soccer match. The turtles' team is slow as molasses while the skunks' team just plain stinks. The game is scoreless with just seconds to go when, suddenly, a centipede—picked up as a ringer by the skunks—rushes onto the field. He gets a pass, dribbles the ball, shoots and scores as the shell-shocked turtles watch the game go by the boards.

Afterwards, the coach of the skunks asks the centipede, "Where have you been all game?"

The centipede answers, "I was stringing up my cleats."

• • •

The Chicken Joke

Colonel Sanders was driving along a rural Kentucky road one day when he spotted a three-legged chicken running down the dusty byway. His professional curiosity was aroused enough to drive along side it for a while, and clock it at 30 mph. "Pretty fast chicken," he thought. "I wonder just how fast it can run?"

He sped up and the chicken kept pace. They were now moving along the road at 45 mph. Sanders sped up again but to his surprise, the chicken was still running ahead of him at 60 mph.

Suddenly, the chicken turned off the road and zoomed down a long driveway leading to a farmhouse.

Sanders followed the chicken and saw a man in the yard with dozens of three legged chickens. Colonel Sanders couldn't believe his eyes. In his excitement, he called out to the farmer "How did you get all these three legged chickens?"

The farmer replied, "I breed 'em. Ya see, we're a family of three and we all like chicken legs. We were always one short, so I started breeding this three legged variety so we could all have our favorite piece."

"That's amazing!" said Colonel Sanders. "How do they taste?"

"Don't rightly know," the farmer drawled. "I ain't caught one yet!"

•

Q: Why does a chicken coop have two doors?
A: Because if it had four doors, it would be a chicken sedan.

•

Q: What do you call a chicken crossing the road?
A: Poultry in motion.

Why did the chicken cross the road?
Answers from various authorities…

Albert Einstein: The chicken didn't necessarily cross the road; the road could be said to have moved laterally under the chicken.

Donald Trump: Hey, a toll road there would make a killing.

President George W. Bush: I would like to unconfusicate the public about this. The chicken was in Iraq and he was crossing the road to escape weapons of mass destruction.

Darth Vader: Because it couldn't resist the power of the dark side.

Paris Hilton: Out on the road? Playing chicken? Sure…Just as soon as I finish this drink.

Neil Armstrong: One small step for a hen; one giant leap for chickenkind.

Donald Trump (again): How about I tear up the road and kill the chicken? Problem solved.

Dick Cheney: Because he's just trying to trick me into shooting another one of my friends in the face.

Ralph Nader: The instances of chickens crossing roads are blown out of all proportion so that auto companies can foist their expensive and unnecessary chicken–avoidance-system off on the public.

Mark Twain: The news of its crossing has been greatly exaggerated.

Al Gore: He never made it. With all the global warming, he was fried as soon as he hit the hot asphalt.

Donald Trump (for the last time): Chicken? Chicken? That reminds me, I have to start working on my comb-over.

The Christmas Joke

Three guys arrive at the Pearly Gates on Christmas Day and St. Peter is in a generous mood. "You can all go in provided you have something that represents this glorious holiday," St. Peter says with a smile.

The first guy pulls his car keys out of his pocket, jingles them, and says, "The keys represent the bells of this wonderful holiday."

"You may go in," says St. Peter.

The next guy pulls out a penlight and says, "This represents the guiding light of the star of Bethlehem."

St. Peter signals him in with a sweep of his hand. The last guy is desperately searching through his pockets but all he can come up with is a pair of panties.

"And just what do those have to do with Christmas?" St. Peter thunders.

"Easy," replies the third guy with a nervous grin. "They're Carol's."

THOUGHTS OF THE THRONE

"Men who consistently leave the toilet seat up secretly want women to get up to go the bathroom in the middle of the night and fall in."
—Rita Rudner

The City Hall Joke

A small town solicits bids for a new city hall and the mayor has the top three contenders come into his office one at a time. "Okay, Mr. Jones," says the mayor to the first bidder. "How much will it cost and how does your figure break down?"

"Two million," replies Jones. "A million for materials and a million for labor."

Jones leaves and the next bidder comes in and answers the same question. "Four million. Two million for materials and two million for labor."

The mayor thanks him and he leaves. Finally, Smith, the third bidder, comes in. The mayor asks him how much the new city hall will cost and he says, "Six million."

"Six million?" sputters the mayor. "That's awfully high. How does that break down?"

"Easy," says Smith. "Two million for me, two million for you and two million for Jones."

The Commuter Joke

Martino lived on Staten Island and commuted to his job in Manhattan. After a string of unfortunate incidents which resulted in him being late several times, he was rushing to work one morning when he saw the ferry already ten feet away from the dock. Determined not to have to wait a half hour for the next boat and be late for work again, Martino ran as fast as he could, jumped the safety chain, dashed up the ramp and made a fantastic flying leap at the vessel. He just barely caught the edge of the deck and hung on by his fingernails until he managed to pull himself on board to the applause of hundreds of fellow commuters. Martino waved and took a slight bow towards his admirers. One of them stepped up, shook his hand and said, "Gee pal, that was really spectacular but you should have waited a few seconds...we're just coming in."

• • •

The Computer Joke

A computer programmer dies and is met by St. Peter at the Pearly Gates. St. Peter gives the programmer the option of spending eternity in Heaven or Hell. The programmer says, "Is it possible to take a quick look at both places before I make up my mind?"

St. Peter says, "Why, of course."

They take a gander at Hell first. Oddly, Hell seems to be a heckuva place...one big party with good food, drink and great atmosphere.

Then St. Peter and the programmer visit Heaven. It's serene to say the least. There are angels sitting on clouds, people in white robes and a general aura of peace, but it doesn't appear to be nearly as much fun as Hell. The programmer tells St. Peter he prefers Hell.

St. Peter grants him his wish and off to Hell the programmer goes.

The computer geek is sorely disappointed to find out that Hell isn't what he thought it was. Hell turns out to be one big ball of fire with people screaming in agony. The programmer registers a complaint to Satan himself. "What's the problem?" asks Satan.

The programmer responds, "I chose to go to Hell rather than Heaven because it looked like it was a terrific place to have a good time, but this is nothing like I was shown."

Satan grins demonically and says, "Aha! That's because you only saw the demo."

• • •

Bytes of Humor

Q: Where do computers go on vacation?
A: To the Big Apple

Q: What's the best way to park a computer?
A: You back it up.

Q: What did the football punter do to the computer?
A: He booted it up.

Q: What happens when you cross a computer with an elephant?
A: I don't know, but you get plenty of memory.

The Confession Joke

A guy goes to confession. He says, "Father, forgive me, for I have sinned. I was skiing when I spotted my boss on the same slope. He didn't recognize me because I was wearing my ski mask. So, I skied over to where he was, gave him a push and roared with laughter as he rolled over and over down the hill, breaking his leg in three places."

"Why are you telling me this again?" asks the priest. "That's the fifth time you've confessed this transgression."

The guy answers, "I know. I just like talking about it."

• • •

The Cop Joke

Riley was speeding down the road at seventy miles per hour. He was pulled over by a cop who said, "Do you know the speed limit is fifty five miles per hour?"

"Yes, officer," replied Riley, looking as innocent as possible, "but I wasn't going to be out that long."

•

In the backwoods of Georgia, a county sheriff observed a truck driver as he pulled off the side of the road, got out and pounded on the sides of his trailer. Thinking it a bit suspicious, the sheriff followed at a discreet distance. A few minutes later, the truck driver pulled off the side of the road again, got out and pounded the sides of his trailer. The third time the truck driver pulled off, the sheriff switched on his lights and sounded the siren. Ambling up to the truck driver, who was again pounding on the side of his trailer, the sheriff drawled, "Now just what do you think you're doing, Boy?"

"Simple, officer," said the truck driver. "I got fifteen tons of canaries in here and the load limit is ten tons so I got to keep some of them flying around."

•

A cop pulled over a Lexus after it had run a stop sign. The officer said, "May I see your driver's license and registration please."

The driver said, "What seems to be the problem?"

"You just ran through a stop sign."

"Oh, man, there wasn't a car in sight."

"Doesn't matter, sir, you're required to come to a complete halt, look both ways, and proceed with caution."

"You're joking."

"This is no joke, sir."

"Look, I slowed down, saw nobody in sight, and then proceeded."

"That's not the point. You're supposed to come to a complete stop. Now please let me see your license and..."

The driver interrupted the cop and said, "Boy, you seem to have a lot of time on your hands. Whatsamatter, all the doughnut shops closed?"

"Ahem, I'll overlook that comment. Let me see your license and registration, now!"

"Okay, but only if you tell me the difference between slowing down and coming to a complete stop."

At this point, the cop had reached his boiling point.

"I can do better than that, sir," explained the officer.

He opened the car door, dragged the driver out and began to beat him over the head with his nightstick. "Now, sir, would you like me to slow down or come to a complete stop?"

•

HERB: I got stopped by a cop the other day.

RALPH: Oh, yeah? What happened?

HERB: He made me get out of the car, walk a straight line, recite the alphabet and then he shined a flashlight in my face and said, "Your eyes look bloodshot. You been drinkin'?"

RALPH: What did you say?

HERB: I said, "Why, no, officer. But your eyes look glazed. Have you been eating donuts?"

•

A man and his wife were out for a drive when a cop pulled them over. As the officer approached the car, the man rolled down his window. The cop said, "Excuse me, sir. Were you aware that you were driving well over the speed limit?"

The driver responded, "Why, no officer, I wasn't aware of that."

With that, his wife exclaimed, "Who are you kidding? You were going at least 20 miles over the limit!"

The cop then asked, "And I noticed you weren't wearing a seat belt. How come?"

He answered, "Well, officer, when I saw you approach the car I figured I'd probably have to get out so I took it off."

His wife then said, "What are you talking about? You never wear a seat belt."

At that point, the cop leaned in and said to the wife, "Does your husband always lie like this?"

"Oh, not always Officer," she replied sweetly, "Only when he's had way too much to drink."

• • •

The Couch Potato Joke

A guy comes home from work, plops himself onto his favorite recliner in the family room, grabs the remote, and flips on the football game on the big screen TV. He yells into the kitchen, "Honey, bring me a cold one before it starts."

THOUGHTS OF THE THRONE

Life is like a movie- since there aren't any commercial breaks, you have to get up and go to the bathroom in the middle of it."

—Garry Trudeau

His wife brings him a can of beer. A few minutes later, he calls out to the wife again, "Honey, bring me another beer before it starts."

Again, his wife brings him a beer. A short time later, he yells a third time, "Honey, hurry up and bring me another beer before it starts."

The wife, now exasperated, marches into the family room and says, "You bum. I've been doing the wash... the dishes... the ironing...and now I'm waiting on you hand and foot!"

As she reads him the riot act, the husband sighs quietly and rolls his eyes, "Oh no, it's started already."

———— • ————

I couldn't find the remote control to the remote control.

—Steven Wright

•

Some guy broke into our house last week.
He didn't even take the TV. He just took the remote control.
Now he drives by and changes channels on us.

—Brian Kiley

• • •

The Counterfeiter Joke

HUEY: My uncle's doing time in the hoosegow for making some big money.

LOUIE: Since when is it a crime to make a lot of money?

HUEY: Since he made it about a half-inch too big.

The Cowboy Joke

Two cowboys are riding along out West when they hear the ominous sound of drums. One of the cowboys says, "I don't like the sound of those drums."

Off in the distance, they hear an Indian yell, "He's not our regular drummer!"

• • •

The Dating Joke

A guy is looking forward to his first date with a girl who lives in a luxurious high-rise apartment. He rings the bell and hears her call out, "I'm not quite ready yet, but come in and make yourself comfortable. I'll be there shortly."

As he sits down in the living room, a miniature poodle comes running in, grabs a ball and plops it down in front of the guy. His date calls out, "Oh, that's Gidget. She loves to play fetch. You can go ahead and play with her while I finish up in here."

 THOUGHTS OF THE THRONE

"I sometimes feel alone and insignificant, especially when people turn out the lights while I'm still in the bathroom."
—Steven Wright

The guy throws the ball and Gidget brings it back to him. He tosses it a little harder and the dog fetches it again. Now the guy throws it even harder. The ball bounces a couple of times, out onto the balcony and over the railing. The dog instinctively chases after it, jumps on a chair and then goes over the railing. The guy is horrified and tiptoes gingerly to the railing to take a peek below.

All of the sudden his date, who turns out to be a real looker, arrives in the living room. The guy steps back inside, they exchange pleasantries and head out on the town. Their date is going along perfectly until the girl asks the fellow, "How did you like Gidget?"

He fumbles for a moment, gulps his glass of wine, takes her hand and says in a soft voice, "Now I'm no expert at this sort of thing, but I must tell you, she did seem a bit depressed."

•

A young Casanova brought a woman home from their first date together. All he asked for was a little goodnight kiss, but she refused his advances, protesting, "I don't do that sort of thing on a first date."

"Well," he replied, "then how about on a last date?"

———— • ————

**Whenever I date a guy, I think, "Is this the man
I want my children to spend their weekends with?"**

—Rita Rudner

The Doctor Joke

Did you hear about the new surgery kit that lets the patient sew up his own incision? It's called Suture Yourself.

•

A guy goes to the doctor and says, "Doc, I just can't do the things around the house that I used to do. What's wrong with me?"

After the exam, the doctor says, "In layman's terms, you're just plain lazy."

"Okay. Now give me a medical term, so I can tell my wife."

•

Two lumberjacks were working in the sawmill one afternoon. Ralph got too close to the saw blade and it cut his arm off. Fred thought that if the limb was put in plastic and taken with the body it could be reattached, so he quickly wrapped up the arm and rushed to the hospital with Ralph. The next day he went to visit his friend and was amazed at what modern medical technology could do when he saw Ralph playing tennis.

A few months later, Ralph and Fred were back to work at the sawmill. Again, Ralph leaned too close to the saw blade and this time his leg was cut off. Fred did the same as last time, wrapping the leg in plastic and rushing Ralph to the hospital. The next day he was thrilled to see Ralph taking a walk. "Isn't medical technology wonderful," he said to himself.

A few weeks later, Ralph and Fred were at work in the sawmill. While trying to lift a log off the ground, Ralph's head came too close to the saw blade and he was decapitated. By now, Fred was an old hand at this. He wrapped up the head and took off for the hospital. The following day he went looking for Ralph, wondering what he might be up to after this latest medical go-around. When he couldn't find him, he called Ralph's doctor to learn of his whereabouts. The doctor shook his head and said, "Oh yes, poor Ralph. I'm sorry to say he didn't make it… We could have saved him but some idiot put his head in a plastic bag and he suffocated!"

———— • ————

**Doctors are crooks. Why do you think they wear gloves?
Not for sanitary reasons – fingerprints.**

—Jackie Mason

•

Doctors are the only people that if they don't find anything wrong they still charge you. You know what you should do? Next time look into your wallet and say you can't find anything either.

—Mark Schiff

The Dog Joke

A dog owner takes his ailing pet to the vet. The vet examines the dog and diagnoses it terminally ill. The dog's owner asks for a second opinion. With that, the vet brings his own kitten into the examining room. The kitten examines the sick dog and shakes his head sadly. The sick dog's owner then asks for one more opinion, so the vet brings in his Labrador retriever. The retriever sniffs the dog all over, licks it in various areas and then shakes his head as well. The pet owner is now sadly convinced of his dog's fate. He asks the vet how much he owes for the exam. The vet says $550. The dog's owner squawks, "How come so much?"

The vet replies, "The exam was only $50. It was an additional $500 for the cat scan and lab test."

•

Two dogs pass by a parking meter. One says to the other, "How do you like that? A pay toilet."

THOUGHTS OF THE THRONE

"The best measure of a man's honesty isn't his income tax return. It's the zero adjust on his bathroom scale."
—Arthur C. Clarke

What do you call a dog that hears voices?
A Shih-Tzu-Phrenic.

•

A classified ad appears in the newspaper for a computer-literate, speed typist who can take dictation and speak more than one language. A dog shows up for an interview. It can type better than a hundred words per minute; its dictation capabilities are superior and it has computer skills second to none. The prospective boss notes all these wonderful things the dog can do and says to the pooch, "You seem perfect for the job, but you know, it does require you to be able to speak another language. What do you have to say about that?"

The dog looks at the would-be employer and says, "Meow!"

•

A pooch goes to a telegraph office. On the form, the dog fills out, "Woof, woof, woof, woof, woof, woof, woof, woof, woof."

The clerk takes a look at the form and says, "You've only filled in nine words here. You're entitled to another woof for the same price."

The dog answers, "But then it wouldn't make any sense."

•

Then there was the girl who named her dog Seiko. Of course, it was a watchdog.

How come the cowboy bought a dachshund?
Someone told him to get a long little doggy.

•

A fellow with a dog act goes to Hollywood for an interview with a talent agent. He brings his little Shih Tzu and St. Bernard into the agent's office. Right away, the Shih Tzu walks to the middle of the office floor and announces to the agent that he'd like to tell a few jokes. Following one hilarious joke after another, the agent says, "Wow, that Shih Tzu's unbelievable!"

The dog owner says, "The Shih Tzu's nothing. The St. Bernard is a ventriloquist!"

•

Then there was the insomniac who was an agnostic dyslexic. He stayed up all night wondering about the meaning of Dog.

———— • ————

My friend George walked his dog, all at once.
Walked him from Boston to Ft. Lauderdale, and said,
"Now you're done."
—Steven Wright

•

Outside of a dog, a book is man's best friend;
inside of a dog, it's too dark to read.
—Groucho Marx

The Donald Joke

Donald Trump visits an old folks' home to mingle with the people and pick up a little good P.R. at the same time. He walks up to a sweet old lady in a wheelchair who smiles at him with an otherwise blank stare.

"Do you know who I am?" says The Donald.

She responds, "No, but if you ask at the desk, they'll tell you."

• • •

The Einstein Joke

Albert Einstein has just finished cementing the sidewalk that leads up to his front door. He's inside reading the newspaper when he hears some loud noises. He looks out the window and sees some kids playing in the still wet cement. Hopping mad, Einstein runs to the door and starts yelling at the kids. His next-door neighbor hears him ranting and raving and calls out, "Calm down, Albert. I thought you liked children!"

"I do," replies Einstein, "but in the abstract, not in the concrete!"

•

In Heaven, Albert Einstein was welcoming his three new cloudmates.

He greeted the first man and asked, "What's your IQ?"

The man answered "198."

"Splendid!" Einstein replied. "We shall discuss the Grand Unification Theory and debate philosophy."

Einstein then asked the next man for his IQ. "139," the man answered.

"Wonderful!" Einstein exclaimed. "We shall spend many happy hours discussing art and music."

Einstein then asked the third man his IQ. The man strained to remember, then brightened up and said, "47."

"47?" Einstein said, scratching his head. "Soooo, how 'bout them Cowboys?"

———— • ————

**Any man who can drive safely while kissing a pretty girl
is simply not giving the kiss the attention it deserves.**

—Albert Einstein

• • •

The Fat Joke

Maybe you've heard about the guy who was so heavy that when he stepped on the digital scale it said, "To be continued."

———— • ————

**It's hard to be famous and struggle with a weight problem.
I was in Baskin Robbins, just looking, and this lady said to me
"Are you Rosie O'Donnell?" I said, "Yes." "I didn't know you were
pregnant." I looked at her and said, "Yes, four and a half months."
She kept asking, "What are you going to name it?"
"I don't know, either Ben or Jerry."**

—Rosie O'Donnell

The Father-In-Law Joke

Hey, how come there are none?

• • •

The Fisherman Joke

A fanatical fisherman calls his doctor and says, "Doc, you gotta help me out. It's an emergency. My baby swallowed a fish hook!"

The doctor says, "Bring him to my office. I'll meet you there."

Before the doctor can even get out the door, the phone rings again and the fisherman says, "Never mind, Doc. I found another fish hook."

•

Did you hear the one about the two dumb guys who went ice fishing?

They caught a whopper but almost drowned trying to fry it.

•

Warren Buffett was on vacation at the beach when he noticed what appeared to be a lazy fisherman sitting leisurely by the water with his pole propped up in the sand and his line cast out into the water.

"Hey, Bud," called Warren. "You're not going to catch any fish like that. You should be at work, anyway."

The fisherman responded, "Oh yeah? Why should I be at work?"

"Because you'll make money and then you can buy a boat which will enable you to catch more fish," said the entrepreneur.

"Why do you think that would be good for me?" questioned the fisherman.

The wealthy financier was becoming a bit irritated answering the fisherman's questions. "That would be good for you because you'd eventually be able to buy a bigger boat and hire other fishermen to work for you," Buffett said.

"Why is that so good for me?" asked the fisherman.

Now Buffett was really annoyed. "Look...you don't seem to get the point. When all is said and done, you could wind up with a whole fleet of fishing boats and amass a great fortune."

"And then what would happen?" asked the fisherman.

Warren, steaming mad, barked, "What would happen?!? You'd become filthy rich and would never have to work again! You could spend the rest of your years sitting on this beach fishing without a care in the world."

The fisherman smiled at the Mr. Buffet and his entourage and said, "And what do you think I'm doing right now?"

Four guys are fishing in a rowboat at the lake. A motorboat speeds by, the boat tips over and the fishermen are thrown into the water. They all swim ashore and take off their wet clothes to dry them over a fire. Soon, two beautiful girls pass by on jet skis. The embarrassed guys wrap their jerseys around their loins – except for one of them, who wraps his shirt around his head and face. After the girls go by, one fisherman turns to the other and says, "What did you do that for?"

"Well, I don't know about you," he answers, "but the people I know usually recognize each other by their faces."

•

Did you hear the one about the three dumb guys who went ice fishing but didn't catch anything?

By the time they cut a hole big enough for the boat to fit in, it was time to go home.

———— • ————

**Dolphin-safe tuna…that's great if you're a dolphin.
What if you're a tuna? Somewhere there's a tuna flopping around
a ship going, "What about me? I'm not cute enough for you?"**

—Drew Carey

The Football Joke

Colts coach Tony Dungy is upset over his team's recent losing streak so he decides to visit Bill Belichick at a New England practice. "Coach, how is it that the Patriots always seem to be on a roll? What's your secret?"

Belichick says, "Watch this." He calls over Tom Brady and says, "Tom, who's your father's brother's nephew?"

Brady responds, "That's easy, coach...me."

Belichick turns to Dungy and says, "That's what it takes, Tony- a smart quarterback. You've got to have a smart QB."

Dungy returns to Indianapolis and at the next Colts' workout calls over Peyton Manning. "Manning," Dungy barks, "Who's your father's brother's nephew?"

Manning looks baffled, then asks, "Uh, can I get back to you on that, Coach?"

Annoyed, Dungy says, "Make it quick."

During practice, Manning asks Marvin Harrison. "Marvin, Coach just asked me a strange question: Who's your father's brother's nephew?"

Harrison answers, "Duuuh, that's simple. It's me."

Later on, Manning catches up with Dungy and says, "Coach, I think I've got it. My father's brother's nephew is Marvin Harrison."

Dungy, exasperated, says, "No, no, no...It's Tom Brady!"

The Frog Joke

A frog wanted to renovate his lily pad so he hopped into a bank to apply for a home equity credit line. He introduced himself to the teller as Kermit Jagger, son of Mick Jagger. When he told her what he wanted, the teller said, "Well, sir, we're going to need proof that you have some collateral in order to get the loan."

With that, the frog produced a small box which the teller opened up. Inside was a tiny souvenir his mother, Bianca, had once brought back to him from a trip. "Oh, I'm sorry," giggled the teller. "This will never do. It's only a knick-knack!"

The frog then tried another teller, only to get the same reaction. "That little knick-knack is worthless. You'll never get a loan trying to use that as collateral."

Undaunted, the frog hopped up the stairs to the boss's office. The sign on the door read "Patricia Black, Bank President." The frog opened the door and found himself face to face with a stern looking lady. "What do you want?" she demanded.

The frog explained that he wanted a loan and showed Patricia Black the knick-knack he had as collateral.

She bellowed, "What the heck is that!?!"

All of the sudden, there was a fierce wind outside, the shutters blew open, and a huge voice from the heavens boomed, "IT'S A KNICK-KNACK, PATTY BLACK, BUT GIVE THE FROG A LOAN! HIS OLD MAN'S A ROLLING STONE."

Old Cornwaithe was playing alone at Pebble Beach one foggy day when he heard a voice from the nearby water hazard. "Hey, Mister," the voice said.

He looked around but saw no one so he resumed his slow creak towards the green. A few seconds later, he heard, "Hey, Mister," once again.

He parted the tall grass at the edge of the water and looked down at a frog perched on a leaf. The frog said, "Yeah, it's me."

"So what do you want, frog?" the old man wheezed.

"Listen, Mister," the frog replied. "I'm really a beautiful princess but an evil witch has cast a spell upon me and turned me into an ugly, slimy frog. All I need is a kiss and I'll turn back into a gorgeous princess. Pick me up, kiss me and then I'm all yours."

With that, the old man scooped up the frog and slipped her in his golf bag. "Hey, Mister," the frog protested. "Aren't you going to kiss me? What about all the fun you can have with me?"

"Thanks just the same," Cornwaithe responded, "but at my age, I'd just as soon have a talking frog."

•

A frog was hopping through a carnival when he landed in the psychic's tent and decided to have his fortune told. Gazing into her crystal ball, the old gypsy said, "I see you with a beautiful young girl who wants to know all about you."

The excited frog asked the fortuneteller, "So will I meet her at a party?"

The old gypsy shook her head and said, "No. Next semester, in her biology class."

•

Bender was fishing one day when he happened to look towards a small clearing nearby and saw a snake with a frog in its mouth. Feeling sorry for the frog, he reached down, gently took the frog from the snake, and set the frog free. But then he felt a pang of guilt for having deprived the snake of his dinner. He looked around for some food, but all he had was a bottle of bourbon. He opened the bottle and shared a few belts with the snake, which slithered off happily.

Ten minutes later, Bender looked over by the clearing again and was surprised to see the snake. This time it was back with two frogs.

• • •

The #$&#@! Joke

What one word can you yell out loud that will make a roomful of little old ladies swear?

"Bingo!"

The Genie Joke

An elderly woman was rocking on her front porch when her dog, Rover, appeared with a lamp in his mouth. The woman took the lamp from the dog and – poof! – a genie appeared. The genie said, "Your three wishes will be my commands."

The old lady thought for a moment and said, "I'd like to be rich."

The genie clapped her hands, turned her rocking chair into solid gold and said, "Your next wish?"

"I would like to be young and beautiful again."

The genie clapped her hands and her wish was granted. She once again was young and beautiful. "And your final wish?" asked the genie.

At that, the dog let out a whimper as though he wanted to be part of this wonderful event. "Well, I haven't enjoyed the company of a good-looking beau in quite some time. Could you possibly make Rover my handsome prince?"

THOUGHTS OF THE THRONE

"My roommate says, 'I'm going to take a shower and shave, does anyone need to use the bathroom?' It's like some weird quiz where he reveals the answer first."

—Mitch Hedberg

The genie once again clapped her hands and then disappeared; Rover had become a gorgeous hunk. His resemblance to Brad Pitt made the woman shiver with excitement. She gave him her best "come hither" look so he nuzzled up to the rejuvenated young maiden and whispered in her ear, "Now aren't you sorry you had me neutered?"

• • •

The Golf Joke

A guy had been stranded on an island for ages. One day as he was walking on the beach, a beautiful woman in a wet suit emerged from the surf. "Hey, cutie pie. Have you been here long?" she asked.

"I reckon about ten years."

"Do you smoke?"

"Oh, what I'd do for a cigarette!" he moaned.

With that, she unzipped a pocket in the sleeve of her wet suit, pulled out a pack of cigarettes, lit one and gave it to him.

"I guess it's been a long while since you've had a drink, huh?"

"You got that right," he said.

She pulled out a flask from another pocket, gave it to him and he anxiously took a long, hard swig.

I bet you haven't played around in a while either," she cooed as she began to unzip the front of her wet suit.

Positively wide-eyed with anticipation, he gasped, "Don't tell me you have a set of golf clubs in there too?"

A minister and his very conservative wife had a great marriage except for his long business trips and lifelong obsession with golf. One day while he was away, she was cleaning and found a box of mementos in the back of the bedroom closet. In it she found three golf balls and $800. That night when he called, she asked him the meaning of the three golf balls. He said, "Well dear, I've been keeping that box for twenty years. I'm ashamed to admit it but so great is my passion for the game of golf that I occasionally swear on the course. Every time I use unsavory language, I penalize myself one golf ball."

Shocked that her husband, a man of the cloth, would ever use four-letter words, the wife was at first taken aback but then thought, "Well, three balls means that he's only cursed three times in 20 years. I suppose that isn't so bad."

"All right dear," she said, "I forgive you for your lapses, but tell me, what's the $800 for?"

"Oh that," answered the minister. "I found a guy who buys golf balls at two bucks a dozen."

•

At a hoity-toity country club with strictly enforced rules of golf, a member saw a guest of the club place his ball five inches in front of the tee markers. The member hurriedly went over to the guest and said, "Sir, I don't know whether you've ever played here before, but we have very stringent rules about placing your tee at or behind the markers before driving the ball."

The guest looked the snooty club member right in the eye and retorted, "First, I've never played here before. Second, I don't care about your rules. And third, this is my second shot."

•

A husband and wife, both golf fanatics, were discussing the future as they sat by a warm fireplace. "Dear," the wife said, "if I died, would you remarry?"

The husband responded, "Well, if something were to happen to you in the near future, I guess so. After all, we're not exactly senior citizens."

"Would you live in this house with her?" the wife asked.

"I would think so."

She continued, "How about my car? Would she get that?"

"I don't see why not."

"What about my golf clubs? Would you give them to her too?"

"Oh, goodness gracious no, never," the husband exclaimed. "She's left-handed."

•

Four old duffers had a Saturday morning 8 o'clock tee time for years.

On one such morning, they noticed a guy watching them as they teed off. At every tee, he caught up with them and had to wait. When they reached the fifth tee, the guy walked up to the foursome and handed them a card which read, "I am deaf and mute. May I play through?"

The old duffers were outraged and signaled to him that nobody plays through their group. He'd just have to bide his time.

On the eighth hole, one of the foursome was in the fairway lining up his second shot. All of the sudden he got bopped in the back of the head by the stinging force of a golf ball. He turned around and looked back at the tee angrily. There stood the deaf mute, frantically waving his arm in the air, holding up four fingers.

•

A miserable, no-good golfer goes to Hell. His eternal punishment is to serve as a caddie for the devil. This is not your normal golf bag toting duty. The devil plays with a hot hand...oven-heated golf clubs and balls. Just as the guy is prepared to caddie for the first time in Hell, he sees a former playing partner, a hideously ugly man, on the first tee with a beautiful woman. The eternally damned caddie mutters out loud, "Why do I have to suffer like this when that guy gets to spend his time with a gorgeous woman like that?"

The devil hears him and says, "Who do you think you are to question that woman's punishment?"

THOUGHTS OF THE THRONE

"We do the 'Real Estate Kneel.'"

–André van Rensburg, Florida Keys exclusive property realtor,
on a method used by men to keep the facilities spotless
when nature calls while hosting an open house

Bushey the Gorilla was making a fortune for his owner. They'd travel around to golf courses and challenge the pro to a round of golf. The hot-shots always accepted the bet, figuring that they could easily beat the muscle-bound primate. That was, until Bushey stepped up to the tee and drove the ball 450 yards. Then they'd usually give up, pay the bet and scamper away to find solace at the Nineteenth Hole. One morning, a top-rated country club pro conceded the bet after the gorilla drove the ball 450 yards to the green. "Just out of curiosity," the pro asked as he forked over the cash, "how does Bushey putt?"

"The same as he drives," said the gorilla's owner. "450 yards."

• • •

The Heaven Joke

A crowd of husbands are about to enter through the Pearly Gates when St. Peter roars, "Hold it right there! I want all of you who were henpecked husbands while on Earth to form a line to my right. The rest of you stand to my left."

All but one husband stands on the henpecked line. St. Peter turns to the guy standing alone and says, "How about you? What's your story?"

He replies sheepishly, "My wife told me to stand here."

•

Three colleges are wooing a high school football star. The player shows up at Ohio State University, where he notices a red telephone on the athletic director's desk. He asks, "What's that phone for?"

"Oh, that," replies the athletic director. "That's the hot line to Heaven."

"Gee, could I borrow it?" asks the football star.

"Sure, but it'll cost you 100 dollars a minute."

"Oh, that's too steep for me."

The player visits the University of Michigan next and sees a blue phone on the athletic director's desk. "What's that blue telephone for?" the player asks the athletic director.

"That's our hot line to Heaven."

The football star asks, "Can I make a call?"

"Yeah, but you'll have to reimburse us 100 dollars a minute."

"Oh, gee. I don't have that kind of money. Thanks anyway."

For the third leg of his college visits, the football player goes to Notre Dame. There, he sees a gold telephone on the athletic director's desk. "What's that phone for?" he asks.

"That's our hot line to Heaven," says the athletic director.

"Mind if I borrow it?"

"Not at all, but we have to keep our costs down so I'm afraid I'll have to ask you to pay for it."

"And how much is that, sir?"

"Five cents a minute."

"Five cents a minute to call Heaven! Wow! How come it's so cheap?" asks the footballer.

The Fighting Irish athletic director responds, "Because it's only a local call."

•

The Pope arrived at the Pearly Gates, where St. Peter took him to his apartment...a small, one-room unit. As the Pontiff was settling in, he looked out the window and saw a limousine pull up in front of a mansion across the heavenly street. A big, burly guy dressed to the nines got out of the limo and was escorted by a couple of female angels into the palatial home. "Wow! Who is that?" asked the Pope.

"Oh, that's Big John McFarland," replied St. Peter. "He was a baseball umpire."

"A baseball umpire?" the Pope said. "My gosh, I was the head of the Roman Catholic Church and all I've got is this tiny room. What magnanimous thing must he have done to be granted with such rewards?"

"To tell you the truth," answered St. Peter, "we have a whole bunch of popes up here, but McFarland is the first umpire we've had in centuries."

•

Heaven and Hell set up a baseball game and St. Peter sounded pretty confident over the phone. "I don't know how you can win," gloated St. Peter. "We have Ruth, Gehrig, Drysdale, Mantle, all the greatest players of all time up here."

"So what?" sneered the devil, "We got all the umpires down here."

The Hell Joke

Satan walked into Duffy's Corner Tap Room and planted his pitchfork firmly on the floor for maximum effect. He cast his evil gaze over the customers, who jumped up and ran out in fear. In seconds, the once crowded bar was empty – save for one old man. The devil strode up to the old-timer and hissed, "Don't you know who I am?"

"Yeah, I know who you are," the old man replied, never looking up from his beer.

"Well, aren't you afraid of me?"

"Afraid of you?" the old man said with disdain. "Why should I be afraid of you? I've been married to your sister for thirty-two years."

•

Smith had a heart attack and passed away at his desk. Naturally, the rest of the office was grief-stricken, but none more so than the boss who realized he had been pushing Smith too hard on the Johnson report.

A few days later, after failing to locate the whereabouts of the Johnson file, the boss went to a psychic and asked her to try and contact Smith in the Great Beyond. The psychic agreed to try, rubbed her crystal ball and, indeed, did manage to get in touch with Smith's spirit. Nervous, the boss asked, "So Smith, how is it where you are?"

"A heck of a lot better than at the office," came the reply.

"Heh-heh, yes I guess so," responded the boss, glad that Smith was happy. "Say, I was wondering before you go back to enjoying Heaven if you could tell me where the Johnson report is?"

"It's in my third drawer," the disembodied voice shot back. "And who said anything about Heaven?"

•

Muggsy and Buggsy had been together in Hell for many, many years. Their eternal job was to shovel coal into the fires side by side.

Suddenly, one day they felt cold air. The air got colder and colder. Snow began to fall. The next thing they knew, there was a blizzard. The snow blanketed the ground and extinguished the fires. Next, a gust of frigid wind froze over the entire surface of Hell! "What the heck is going on here?" Muggsy wondered out loud.

Buggsy answered, "I don't know for sure, but I have a hunch that the Bills just won the Super Bowl."

———— • ————

People in Hell: Where do they tell someone to go?
—Red Skelton

The Hillbilly Joke

A family of three from bucolic parts unknown was touring New York City. They walked into the Empire State Building together and the mother paused to view the magnificent art in the lobby. The father and son went on ahead and, for the first time in their lives, saw an elevator. They were perplexed by the sideways sliding doors and couldn't imagine what the little room was for. Just then, an elderly woman walked up and hit the button. The doors opened and she stepped in. The boy and his dad watched as the doors closed and the little round numbers went higher and higher. Then they paused and dropped back down. A little bell sounded, the doors opened and out stepped a voluptuous, eighteen-year old beauty that any country boy would be proud to have as a kissin' cousin. The father was simply amazed and, keeping his eye on the elevator, tapped the boy on the shoulder. "Billy-Bob," he said intently, "go get your mother."

•

A hillbilly taking a walk comes to a river and sees another hillbilly on the opposite bank. He yells, "Hey, how do I get to the other side?"

The other hillbilly looks up and down the river and hollers back, "You are on the other side."

The Hockey Joke

A clerk working part-time in a grocery store was having a difficult time with a customer who kept insisting on buying only half a head of lettuce. Finally, the employee went to his manager and said, "Boss, there's some idiot in the produce department who wants only a half a head of lettuce."

Then, out of the corner of his eye he saw the customer standing directly behind him so he quick-wittedly said, "And this gentleman would like to buy the other half."

After the customer was satisfactorily taken care of, the manager praised the clerk for his quick-thinking and asked, "Where are you from?"

He replied proudly, "From Montreal, the city of hockey players and loose women."

The manager shot him a dirty look and growled, "Hey, my wife's from Montreal!"

"Which team?" asked the clerk.

The Hook, Line and Stinker Joke

George had a miserable time of it on the lake, with not so much as a single nibble all day. On his way home, he stopped at the fish market and ordered catfish. "Pick out four big ones and throw them at me," he told the fish monger.

"Why would you want me to throw them at you?"

"Because I want to be able to tell my wife that I caught them," replied George.

"In that case, I think you should take the salmon."

"Why's that?" George asked a bit perplexed.

"Because your wife came in and said that if you stopped by, she'd prefer salmon for dinner tonight."

•

A fishing trawler goes down, leaving only one survivor. Eventually, he washes ashore on a remote island inhabited by cannibals. They capture him and tie him to a stake, where they proceed to nick him with their spears and drink his blood. This goes on for two weeks. The guy can't take it any longer and asks to see the chief. When the cannibal leader arrives, the guy says, "Look, chief...either let me go or kill me. I'm tired of being stuck for the drinks."

———— • ————

I went fishing with a dotted line. I caught every other fish.
—Steven Wright

The Horse Joke

A guy loves betting on the ponies. Every dollar he can beg, borrow or steal is spent at the track. One day his wife becomes very ill and is rushed to the hospital. The inveterate gambler goes to a friend and says, "Please, you've gotta help me. I'm gonna need some money to pay for my wife's hospital bills."

"I'm not loaning you anything, pal," his friend remarks. "You'll just blow it all on the horses."

"Don't be ridiculous," the guy huffs. "Gambling money, I got."

•

A 44-year old man, who was born on April 4th, has been married for four years, has four kids, earns $44,444.44 a year, and whose lucky number is four, gets a racing tip from a buddy. He's told that a horse named Four Leaf Clover will be running in the fourth race in the number four spot at the local track that evening. The man hurries to the bank, withdraws $4,444.44, goes to the races and bets it all on Four Leaf Clover in the fourth. Sure enough, the horse comes in…fourth.

•

Doc, I need help," says Mort to the psychiatrist. "It may sound strange, but I keep thinking that I'm a horse."

"I think I can cure you," the psychiatrist answers, "but it's going to take some time and it's going to be extremely expensive."

"Money's not a problem, Doc. I just won the Kentucky Derby."

•

"I can't believe my rotten luck," moaned Mulligan. "I haven't had a winning horse in more than two months."

"Hey, maybe you should try out my system," said Hoolihan. "It's worked pretty well for me lately."

"What system is that?" asked Mulligan.

"Well," answered Hoolihan, "it's pretty simple. Every day that I plan on going to the track, that morning I go to church and pray for ten minutes. I've had at least two winners a day since I've been doing that."

Mulligan was ready to try anything so, sure enough, the next morning he went to church and prayed for half an hour. Then it was off to the racetrack. At the end of the day, he ran into Hoolihan. "That system of yours is hooey," Mulligan complained. "I went to church this morning, prayed three times as long as you do and didn't have a single winner all afternoon."

"Where did you go to church?" asked Hoolihan.

"I went to the one on Peach Street," said Mulligan.

"You idiot!" exclaimed Hoolihan. "That church is for trotters."

The Hotel Joke

Visitor: Does this hotel have a swimming pool?

Desk Clerk: Yes, sir. Swimming is allowed all day except for between two and three in the afternoon.

Visitor: Why's that?

Desk Clerk: Because that's when we wash the sheets.

• • •

The Insurance Joke

Three businessmen, who had just met, were getting massages together at a swank resort in Hawaii. The first guy said, "I had a horrible fire- destroyed everything. Now the insurance company is paying for everything and that's why I'm here."

The second businessman said, "I had a terrible explosion which wiped me out. Now the insurance company is paying for everything and that's why I'm here."

The third businessman said, "What a coincidence. I had a tremendous flood that destroyed everything. Now the insurance company is paying for everything and that's why I'm here."

Confused, the other guys turned to him and said, "Flood? How do you start a flood?"

Gina Borelli called her insurance agent to inform him that her house had burned down. "I had the place insured for a quarter-million dollars, so I'll be over to pick up the money."

"Hold your horses, Mrs. Borelli," cautioned her insurance agent. "That's not how it works. We'll determine the value of your home and then provide you with a new one of comparable worth."

"Oh," said Mrs. Borelli, a bit disappointed. "In that case, cancel the policy on my husband."

• • •

The Job Joke

A guy applies for a sales position with a big financial investment firm. While he's waiting for the interview, he strikes up a nice conversation with the receptionist, who at one point says, "Look, you seem like a nice guy. Let me give you a tip. My boss is very sensitive about the fact that he doesn't have any ears. At some point, he's going to ask you if you notice anything odd about him. Whatever you do, don't make any mention of the ears."

The guy thanks the receptionist for the advice and goes in for the interview. Well, the boss is very impressed with the guy's resume, his knowledge of the world of finance and his personable demeanor. But sure enough, at one point the boss says, "Tell me. Do you notice anything different about me?"

The guy looks at the boss and responds, "Well, now that you mention it, I can tell you're wearing contact lenses."

"That's amazing," says the boss. "I like perceptiveness in my employees. But how on earth did you know I wear contacts?"

"Easy. You'd be wearing glasses if you had any ears."

•

How come you never hear about gruntled employees?

•

ARNIE: My girlfriend lost her job.

BARNEY: What kind of work did she do?

ARNIE: She was a proofreader in the M&Ms factory.

BARNEY: What happened?

ARNIE: She kept throwing out all the 'W's.

•

A freckle-faced Florida teen had a job bagging groceries at an Orlando supermarket. He hated what he did, but worked hard at it. One day, the store installed a machine to squeeze fresh orange juice and was looking for someone to run it. The boy was eager for the new position but the boss turned him down cold. When asked why, the manager explained, "Sorry, kid. Everybody knows baggers can't be juicers."

The Judge Joke

The courtroom was packed as the judge was explaining to the jury that a witness was not necessarily untruthful solely because he changed his statement from one he had previously given to the police. "For instance," the judge said, "when I came to court today, I was sure I had my gold pocket watch with me. But then I recalled that I left it in the valet on my bedroom dresser."

After the day's session, the judge returned home. His wife quizzically asked, "Why the urgency for your watch? Isn't sending four men to get it a bit of overkill?"

"What are you talking about?" said the judge. "I didn't send anyone for the watch. What did you do?"

"I gave it to the first guy who came," she said. "After all, he knew just where it was."

THOUGHTS OF THE THRONE

"My kids always perceived the bathroom as a place where you wait it out until all the groceries are unloaded from the car."
—Erma Bombeck

The Knock-Knock Joke

Knock knock!

Who's there?

Interrupting cow.

Interrupti...

MOOOOOOOOOOOOOOOOOOOOOOOOOOOOOOOO!

————— • —————

Cow with no legs is ground beef.
—Bathroom Graffiti

• • •

The Lawyer Joke

A guy walks into a lawyer's office and asks, "What are your rates? "Two hundred dollars for three questions," answers the lawyer. "That's a pretty hefty charge, isn't it?" retorts the man. "Maybe," the lawyer responds. "What's your final question?"

•

Terrorists raided the annual attorneys' convention in New York and held all the lawyers hostage. They threatened that until their demands were met, they'd release a lawyer every hour.

•

Q: What did the lawyer name his daughter?

A: Sue.

A guy walks into a crowded room and shouts, "All lawyers are idiots!"

A fellow in the back of the room yells, "I resent that remark."

The guy says, "Why? Are you a lawyer?"

"No, I'm an idiot."

• • •

The Little Johnny Joke

"Hey, Grandpa, can you make a noise like a frog?" asked Little Johnny.

"Why do you want me to do that, Johnny?"

"Because Mom said when you croak, we're goin' to Disney World!"

•

Little Johnny was in his backyard filling in a hole when his neighbor asked, "What are you doing, Johnny?"

"My goldfish died and I've just buried him," answered Johnny. The sympathetic neighbor said, "That seems like an awfully big hole for a goldfish."

Little Johnny replied, "That's because he's inside your stupid cat."

THOUGHTS OF THE THRONE

Show me a nation whose national beverage is beer, and I'll show you an advanced toilet technology."
—Paul Hawkins

Little Johnny's mother, in an attempt to get him to stop sucking his thumb, told him that if he continued to do so his stomach would get bigger and bigger until it burst.

Later that day, they went to the supermarket, where Johnny saw a very pregnant woman. Noticing that he was staring at her, the woman said, "You don't know me. You shouldn't be staring at me."

Johnny replied, "I may not know you, but I know what you've been doing."

•

A kindergarten teacher was reading the "Three Little Pigs" to her class. She came to the part of the story where the first pig was trying to gather the building materials for his home. She read, "...And so the pig went up to the man with the wheelbarrow full of straw and said, 'Excuse me sir, but may I have some of that straw to build my house?'" The teacher paused and then asked the class, "And what do you think that man said?"

Little Johnny raised his hand and said, "I know. He said, 'Holy crap! A talking pig!'"

•

Little Johnny was in his kindergarten class when the teacher asked the kids what their dads did for a living. The usual jobs came up-fireman, salesman, accountant, policeman- but Johnny was uncharacteristically shy about giving an answer. Finally, the teacher said, "Johnny, how about you? What does your father do for a living?"

Johnny murmured, "My dad's a circus freak who bites the heads off small animals."

The startled teacher quickly ended that segment of class and sent the other kids off to do some coloring. Then, she took little Johnny aside and said, "Is that really true about your father?"

"No," said Johnny, "but I was afraid the other kids would make fun of me if I said that he's really a lawyer."

•

Little Johnny dreamed of going to the zoo and pestered his parents about it day in and day out. Finally his mother nagged his reluctant father into taking Johnny to the zoo for the day.

"So how was it?" his mother asked when they got home.

"Terrific," the father replied. "We had a great time. I was surprised at how much I enjoyed it."

"Is that true, Johnny?" his mom asked. "Did Daddy really have as good a time as you?"

"Yeah, Mom... He sure did- especially when one of the animals came running home at thirty to one!"

THOUGHTS OF THE THRONE

"My family tree was chopped down and they made the lumber into toilet paper. We've never been closer."
—Barry Steiger

At the ripe old age of three, Little Johnny began playing Superman. Every day, his mommy would pin a bright red bath towel on his blue t-shirt and he'd become the superhero. Well, when it came time to enroll for kindergarten, the teacher was interviewing the caped Little Johnny and his mother. When the teacher asked him his name, Johnny answered politely, "Superman."

The teacher smiled at Johnny and his mother and asked his name again. Again, Johnny said, "Superman."

Now, the teacher was a bit concerned, so she said, "I will have to have your real name for my records."

Johnny bent over and whispered in her ear, "Clark Kent."

•

JOHNNY: I ate a submarine sandwich for lunch and I think I'm going to be sick.

MOTHER: What makes you say that?

JOHNNY: It's starting to surface.

• • •

The Lottery Joke

A guy wins the lottery with a $1 ticket. He goes to claim his $20 million jackpot and demands the money all at once. The lottery representative says, "Sorry sir, it doesn't work that way. You get a million up front and the rest is paid over the next nineteen years."

The disgruntled fellow argues, "Oh, no. I want all my money right now! I won it and I want it."

Again, the agent explains that he'll get a million immediately and the rest over time. Now furious with the lottery agent, the guy yells, "Look, I want my money! If you're not going to give me my $20 million right now, then I want my dollar back!"

•

Every day this guy prays to God to let him win the lottery. He keeps promising to do all sorts of good deeds if God will only let him win the jackpot. Week after week he prays but never wins. Finally, one day he's talking to God and says, "I'm a good man. I've been praying faithfully. Can't you allow me to win the lottery?"

A booming voice from the heavens answers, "You gotta buy a ticket!"

• • •

The Marriage Joke

After a knock-down, drag-out fight, a wife complained to her husband, "You know, I was a fool when I married you!" He replied, "Yeah, sweetheart, but I was in love and didn't notice it."

•

An elderly retired couple were discussing their future. "What will you do if I should die before you?" the husband asked.

The wife thought for a moment and replied, "Oh, I guess I'd look for a situation where I could share a place with two or three single or widowed women. I think I'd prefer them to be younger than I am since I'm still very active... What would you do if I die first?"

He replied, "I guess I'd do the same thing."

A husband and wife were vacationing on a cross country trip. As they passed through a rural area, they began to quibble about the pronunciation of a small town. Finally, they decided to stop at a fast food place to ask one of the local folk how to pronounce it. They walked into the restaurant, placed an order with the waitress, and the wife asked, "Could you please tell us where we are and, if you don't mind, say it real slow?"

The waitress said, "Listen very closely... M-c-D-O-N-A-L-D-S."

•

Three guys are on their lunch break, talking about their wives. Two of them are bragging about how they're the "man of the house" while the third remains silent. After a while, one of the guys says to the third fellow, "You've been pretty quiet, pal. What's the matter, does your wife boss you around?"

The third guy says, "Let me tell you guys something. Just the other night, my wife came to me crawling on her hands and knees."

The first two guys look at him astonishingly and one says, "What was the reason for that?"

"She said, 'Get out from under that bed and fight like a man you little weasel.'"

•

Harvey had been in and out of a coma for several months. His wife stayed by his side every moment. One evening he came to, and called her over to his bed. She sat by him and tears welled up in her eyes as he said, "My darling, you were with me all along, always at my side. When I got fired, you were there. When I got charged with tax evasion, you were there. When my business went bankrupt, you were there. And now, my health is failing and you are here. You know what?"

"What my dear? Tell me what," she implored, her voice cracking with emotion.

Harvey drew his last gasp of air and replied, "I'm beginning to think you're bad luck."

•

A couple having a candlelit dinner to celebrate their silver wedding anniversary were surprised by the sudden appearance of the Fairy Godmother. "You have had such a wonderful relationship all these years that I will reward you with anything you ask," she announced.

The woman said, "I always wanted to take a romantic around-the-world cruise with my husband."

The Fairy Godmother waved her wand and -poof!- two tickets appeared in the woman's hand. Then it was the husband's turn. "I hate to say this, but you only get a wish like this once and I always wanted to be married to a woman about twenty-five years younger than me."

THOUGHTS OF THE THRONE

"At a formal dinner party, the person nearest death should always be seated closest to the bathroom."
—George Carlin

His wife was crushed, totally crestfallen. "Sorry, Hon, but that's what I want."

"But Dear," the wife pleaded, "don't leave me."

"Forget it," he snorted, "I want a wife twenty-five years younger than me and that's that."

He then signaled the Fairy Godmother to make it so. The Fairy Godmother nodded, waved her wand and -poof!- the man got his wish. He was now ninety-five years old.

•

Marriage is a relationship in which one person is always right, and the other is a husband.

•

If a man says something in the middle of the forest and there is no woman around to hear him...is he still wrong?

———— • ————

Marriage is really tough because you have to deal with feelings and lawyers.

—Richard Pryor

My wife is the sweetest, most tolerant, most beautiful woman in the world. This is a paid political announcement.

—Henny Youngman

• • •

The Merger Joke

Did you hear that FedEx is merging with UPS? It's going to be called FedUp.

•

The former star of *Happy Days* and *Laverne & Shirley* has formed a conglomerate to purchase both Marshall's and JC Penney. The new mega-store is going to be called Penny Marshall.

•

Stop and Shop is merging with A&P. It's going to be called Stop and Pee.

• • •

The Monastery Joke

Brother Joseph called all the monks together and said to them, "I must tell you all something. We have a case of gonorrhea in the monastery."

"Praise Heaven," said an elderly monk at the back. "I was getting really tired of drinking that crap we make."

The Mother-In-Law Joke

Q: What do you have when your mother-in-law drives off a cliff in your brand new Mercedes?

A: Mixed emotions.

———— • ————

There are only three basic jokes, but since the mother-in-law joke is not a joke but a very serious question, there are only two.

—George Ade

•

Be kind to your mother-in-law, and if necessary pay for her board at some good hotel.

—Josh Billings

• • •

The Office Joke

During a pre-employment screening, the company psychologist wanted to check the applicant's grasp on reality. "Now tell me, son," began the shrink. "If you looked out that window right now and saw a battleship coming up the middle of the street, what would you do?"

"I'd jump in my submarine, fire a torpedo and sink it."

"Where would you get the submarine?"

"The same place you got your battleship."

Bert worked for Conglomo Enterprises for forty years. Every evening without fail, he would leave his office with a box tucked under his arm and tip his hat to Farnsworth, the watchful security guard. After several decades of this, it was time for Bert to retire and, as was his habit, he walked through the lobby precisely at five with a box tucked under his arm. When he got to the security station, Farnsworth stopped him. "Bert, I heard you retired today and I have something to ask you. Every night I've seen you go out of here with a box under your arm that you didn't have when you came in. It was driving me crazy so we inventoried the office supplies time and again and nothing was missing. We also accounted for every piece of stock, equipment and even toilet paper. I know you've been stealing something and it's been extremely frustrating to me. Bert, we've known each other for a long time and I won't be seeing you again. Just between you and me, what have you been pilfering all these years?"

Bert smiled and patted the package under his arm as he answered, "Boxes."

•

"Why are you so late?" growled the boss.

"Well, boss...the alarm clock woke up everybody but me this morning."

"Whaddya mean by that?"

"There are seven people in our family and the alarm was set for six."

An enterprising young man decided to start his own business. He leased a posh, top-floor office in the big city. The first day he was in the office he was sitting at the desk when he saw another guy come into the reception room. Trying to look as executively important as possible, the entrepreneur picked up the telephone and got into a one-way big deal business conversation. After throwing around seven-figure digits for the make-believe deal, he hung up the phone and inquired of the visitor, "What can I do for you?"

'Well, if you're finished," the guy answered, "I've come to install your phone."

•

The CEO of a match manufacturing company receives a call from the President of the United States. The President tells the CEO that he's going to be given the Presidential Medal of Patriotism and that he should report to the Rose Garden the next day. The CEO has no clue as to why he should receive such a distinction, but he shows up the next day at the White House. He's standing with the President who, as the CEO is presented with the medal, says, "Terrorists tried to burn down one of our most strategic military facilities last week but the Evil Doers' mission failed."

The CEO interjects, "But I don't understand, Mr. President. What does that have to do with me getting this medal?"

The President answers, "The matches wouldn't light."

•

"How come you're an hour late this morning, Riley?" demanded the boss. "It was so slippery outside, that for every step I took, I'd slip back two."

"Well, then how did you manage to get here at all?" questioned the boss.

Riley responded, "I finally gave up and headed back for home."

•

And then there was the less-than-stellar businessman who thought Dunn and Bradstreet was an intersection.

•

Smith and Ryan went into business together and opened a whole-sale leather goods outlet. They were doing quite well until a huge recession came along and they found themselves with thousands and thousands of belts, wallets and jackets left in stock with nary a customer. Just as they were about to declare bankruptcy, a guy walked in and introduced himself as the senior buyer for a large menswear chain in England. "By any chance is any of your stuff made of alligator leather? I'll take anything and everything made in alligator skin. It's caught Great Britain by storm."

That was just the ticket for Smith and Ryan, as a huge chunk of their inventory was made of alligator leather. Smith said to the Brit, "If the price is right, I think we can work out a deal."

After some haggling, a deal was made and all parties signed on the dotted line. As he was leaving, the Brit said, "I have to caution you, guys. I must get the authority from my home office for a deal that's this big. I'll tell you what... Today is Tuesday. If you don't get a fax from me by Friday, the deal stands."

For the next few days, Smith and Ryan sweated it out but there were no faxes at all; however, on Friday, as the day was about to end and the partners would be in the money, lo and behold, the fax phone began ringing. Smith practically fainted as Ryan went over to the fax machine and ripped off the message. Ryan jumped for joy as he yelled out to Smith, "Great news…Your house burnt down!"

• • •

The Old Geezers Joke

Sam and Moe were rocking on the porch at the retirement home. Having talked about everything under the sun, Sam was grasping for a new topic of conversation. "Tell me, Moe, have you read Marx?" Sam asked.

"Yes," replied Moe. "And, you know, I think it's the wicker chairs."

•

Three old geezers were sitting on a bench in New York City's Central Park. The one in the middle was reading a newspaper while the other two were pretending to fish. A policeman on the beat watched them as they baited imaginary hooks, cast their lines and reeled in their fake catches. "Do you know these two?" the cop asked the guy reading the paper.

"Sure. They're buddies of mine."

"Well, they're disturbin' the other people. You better get them outta here!"

"Yes, officer," said the guy, and with that he furiously began rowing.

The Olympics Joke

At the summer Olympic Games, a girl bumped into a guy carrying an eight-foot long stick. "Excuse me," said the girl, "but are you by any chance a pole vaulter?"

"Nein, I'm a German, but how did you know my name is Valter?"

•

Three guys desperately want to get into the Olympic stadium but the Games are sold out so they decide to pose as athletes. The first guy picks up a long piece of pipe, walks up to the athletes' entrance and says to the guard, "I'm a pole vaulter." The guard lets him in.

The second guy appears with a manhole cover and says, "Discus thrower." He's also allowed in.

The third guy shows up carrying a roll of barbed wire. Confused, the guard looks up and the guy says, "Fencing."

——— • ———

**That silver medal at the Olympics, that's something, isn't it?
You get gold, you've won. You get bronze, 'Well, at least
I got something.'
But silver is basically saying, 'Of everyone that lost, you were the best.
No one lost ahead of you; you are the very best loser.'**

—Jerry Seinfeld

THOUGHTS OF THE THRONE

*"I'm not at the point where I'd feel safe in a house alone.
I would be really scared. I'm the kind of person that when
I get up to go use the bathroom I have this big long hallway,
and I just know someone's going to jump out and get me."*
—Britney Spears

The Parking Lot Joke

The scene was a shopping mall just before Christmas and Mrs. Dentzel was waiting for another car to pull out of its space. Just as the car cleared the spot, a teenager in a Corvette swung around the corner and stole it. "You saw me waiting there for that space," Mrs. Dentzel yelled out. "I even had my signal on."

"Sorry, that's what happens when you're young and fast," the kid sneered.

With that, Mrs. Dentzel backed up and then gunned her classic Mercedes into the Corvette, ramming it over and over again until the fiberglass body was nothing but a crumpled heap.

"Hey, what'd you do that for?" the teen whined.

"Sorry," replied Mrs. Dentzel with a sweet smile. "That's what happens when you're old and rich."

———— • ————

My father would say things that make no sense, like, 'If I were the last person on earth, some moron would turn left in front of me.'
—Louie Anderson

The Parrot Joke

Bidder: I'm here to pick up the parrot I bought at tonight's auction, but before I pay the two thousand bucks, I want to make sure the bird can talk.

Auctioneer: Talk? Who do you think was bidding against you?

• • •

The Pope Joke

Why did the Pope cross the road?

He crosses everything.

• • •

The Priest Joke

Father Flanagan was playing Bingo at a friend's parish. The first game, he needed 49 to win diagonally. It came up 50 and someone else won. Sitting alongside, Sister Margaret heard the priest mutter, "Hoover" under his breath.

Next game, he was one off again and mut'tered, "Hoover."

He got lucky on the next game with a win straight down the B column.

"Praise be to God," he exclaimed.

Bad luck returned the next game and, once more, Father Flanagan snorted "Hoover!"

Sister Margaret couldn't contain her curiosity any longer. She asked, "Father, whenever you lose a game you mutter 'Hoover.' I was just wondering why?"

"Because," Father Flanagan replied with a twinkle in his eye, "It's the biggest dam I know."

•

One day on the links, a man was separated from his companions for a few moments and the devil took the opportunity to appear to him. "Say, friend," the devil said in his best used car salesman smile, "how'd you like to make a hole-in-one to impress your buddies?"

"What's the catch?" asked the fellow suspiciously.

"It'll shorten your love life by five years," grinned the devil.

"Hmmm. All right, I'll do it," agreed the man.

He then went on to make one of the most spectacular shots ever and aced the hole. A few minutes later the devil approached the man on the following tee. "How'd you like to go for two in a row?"

"At what cost?" asked the man.

"This'll shorten your love life by ten years."

"You drive a tough bargain, but okay," replied the golfer, who then strode to the tee and sent a 310 yard beauty right into the cup.

At the next tee, the devil appeared once again. "This is a once in a lifetime offer. If you ace this one, it'll be three straight holes-in-one. It's never been done before in the history of the world. But it's gonna cost you another twenty years off your love life."

"Let's go for it," said the man.

He proceeded to dazzle everyone by hitting the ball from behind his back, sending it over a huge pond onto the green and right into the hole. It was such an amazing shot that even the devil himself applauded.

And that's the story of how Father O'Malley got into the *Guinness Book of World Records.*

———— • ————

Celibacy is not hereditary.

—Guy Goden

• • •

The "Q&A" Joke

Q: What do you call a retired comedian from Richmond?
A: A Virginia ham.

•

Q: How did the girl break up with the tractor salesman?
A: She sent him a John Deere letter.

•

Q: What do old bowling balls become?
A: Marbles for elephants.

•

Q: What do you call a dead Frisbee?
A: A Friswas.

•

Q: What do you get when you cross a hen with a bookmaker?
A: A chicken that lays odds.

The Rabbit Joke

A rabbit hopped into a butcher shop and asked, "Do you have any carrots?"

"No," said the butcher.

The next day the rabbit showed up and said, "Have any carrots?"

"If I told you once, I told you twice- The answer is NO," said the butcher.

The following day the rabbit appeared again and said, "Got any carrots?"

The butcher angrily replied, "N-O, NO! And if you come back in here again and ask for carrots, I'll hammer you to the wall by your ears!"

The next day the rabbit came back and asked, "Do you have any nails?"

"No," said the butcher.

"Good ... Do you have any carrots?"

•

What do you have if you've got 10 rabbits in a row and they all move back one step?

A receding hare-line.

The Ranch Joke

A city slicker, who always fancied himself owning a cattle ranch out West, finally earned enough dough to make his dream come true – a five hundred acre spread in Montana. A friend from back East was visiting him one day and asked, "So what did you name the ranch?"

Well, that was a tough one," answered the new cowboy. "The cowhands and me couldn't agree on anything. We finally settled on calling it the Double R Lazy S Triple Horseshoe, Four-Diamond Bar – 7 Lucky – 11 Ranch."

"Golly!" exclaimed his friend. "That's a mouthful. Say- where are all the cows?"

"So far," the city slicker shrugged sadly, "none of them survived the branding."

•

A Texas rancher took a trip to see a distant cousin in Australia. Visiting his farm, the Texan scoffed at the ten thousand acre wheat field. "Heck, we got posy patches bigger than that back home."

The Aussie next showed him the longhorn herds, the pride of the territory. "You call them longhorns?" the Texan crowed. "Heck, we'd have a couple of them just to make shish kabobs at one of our barbecues back home."

Just then, a few hundred kangaroos came hopping through and stampeded over the Texan. After they passed, the Aussie farmer helped the Texan to his feet. "What in blazes were those critters?" the Texan asked, trying to regain his balance.

"What's the matter, Mate?" the Aussie replied. "Don't you have any grasshoppers in Texas?"

The Salesman Joke

A traveling salesman came up to an old man rocking on his front porch but stopped short when he spotted a rather large and fierce looking dog. "Excuse me, sir," the salesman called out. "Does your dog bite?"

"Nope," the old man answered.

The salesman straightened his phony grin and confidently strode up the steps. With that, the dog jumped at him and buried his teeth in the salesman's backside. "Hey, I thought you said your dog didn't bite," complained the salesman.

The old man looked up and said, "It ain't my dog."

•

A clothing salesman, who just returned from a vacation in Italy, is talking with one of his cohorts. He says, "The best part of our trip was meeting the Pope."

"Wow. You met the Pope?"

"Yep... sure did."

"What sort of man is he?"

"A forty-two long."

•

A businessman went to a hunting lodge and, supplied with a dog named Salesman, bagged a record number of birds. When he returned the next year, he asked for Salesman once again. Again, a record number of birds.

The third year he was back again, anticipating another banner hunting trip with Salesman, but the lodge manager said, "The hound ain't no good anymore."

"What happened!" asked the disappointed businessman. "Was he injured?"

"No," the manager replied. "Some danged fool came down here and called him 'Sales Manager' for a week instead of Salesman. Now all he does it sit on his tail and bark."

———— • ————

I had a cool job. I sold "No Soliciting" signs door to door.

—Buzz Nutley

• • •

The Skydiving Joke

As a fierce hurricane moved across the Florida peninsula, an orange grower was securing his property when he looked up and saw a man parachuting down into one of his groves. Driving his tractor a half-mile out into the field to rescue him, the grower yelled above the howling wind, "That was a crazy thing you did, parachuting down in a hurricane."

"I didn't parachute down in a hurricane," the man answered. "I went up in a tent!"

•

Eyewitless News reporter Alana Airhead had her story for the first night of Sweeps Weeks. The roving reporter was doing a feature on Blind Parachuting. She managed to arrange an interview with a local sightless man who went skydiving every week.

"Tell me, Mr. Jordan," she purred sweetly as the cameras rolled. "How do you manage it?"

He answered that he got a lot of help from his friends. "They place me in the door and push me out at the right time. My hand is already on my rip cord."

"But how do you know when you are coming close to the ground?" the reporter asked.

"I can smell the trees when I'm still about 500 feet in the air," he answered enthusiastically.

"But how do you know when to pull up your legs for the landing?" the reporter asked in bewilderment.

"Oh, that's easy," he smiled, "the dog's leash goes slack."

———— • ————

If at first you don't succeed, stay away from skydiving.

—Milton Berle

• • •

The School Joke

Jimmy woke up and said, "Mom, I don't want to go to school today."

"But you have to go to school," she replied.

"I'll give you two reasons why I'm not going to school," he asserted. "One: they don't like me, and two: I don't like them."

"And I'll give you two reasons why you have to go," his mother answered. "One: you're 39 years old, and two: you're the teacher!"

The Seeing Eye Dog Joke

A blind fellow walks into a department store with his Seeing Eye dog. He's whipping the dog around over his head by its tail. A department store manager comes over and says, "Excuse me, sir. Can I help you?"

"No," replies the blind man, "I'm just looking."

•

Norman was walking his dog when the seductive aroma of an Italian restaurant he was passing called him to lunch. He decided to take his Chihuahua into the restaurant with him, so he donned dark glasses and tapped his way into the establishment. After seeing the man, a waiter remarked, "Hey Mister – you can't bring a dog in here."

Norman indignantly replied, "It just so happens that I'm blind and this is my Seeing Eye dog."

"I don't think so. That dog is a Chihuahua."

"What?" cried Norman. "They gave me a Chihuahua?"

• • •

The Sex Joke

An 8-year-old girl asked, "Daddy, what is sex?"

The surprised father was taken aback but decided that if she was old enough to ask the question, she was old enough to get an answer. After telling her all about the birds and the bees, he said, "Why do you ask?"

Still a little wide-eyed, the little girl replied, "Mom told me to tell you that dinner would be ready in just a couple of secs."

The Shrink Joke

A guy goes to a psychiatrist and says, "My wife thinks I'm crazy because I like plaid socks." "That's not so strange," replies the doctor. "As a matter of fact, I kind of like them, too."

"Really?" exclaimed the patient, excited to find a sympathetic ear. "Do you like yours with chocolate fudge or Hollandaise sauce?"

•

A guy goes to a psychiatrist and says, "Doc, you gotta help me."

The shrink says, "What's your problem?"

He says, "Oh, it's not me. It's my wife. She thinks she's a lawn mower."

"How long has this been going on?" asks the doctor.

"Oh, for about a year and a half."

The doctor says, "Why didn't you bring her in here sooner?"

"I couldn't, Doc. The last guy who borrowed her didn't return her for six months."

•

If somebody who has multiple personalities threatens to kill himself, is it considered a hostage situation?

•

After receiving the diagnosis from his psychiatrist, the patient says, "Doc, I know you say I have a split personality, but is it okay for me to get married?"

"Sure ... Who are you planning to marry?"

"The Jones twins."

> **Dr. Phil is hiding something.**
> **Otherwise, why wouldn't he use his last name?**
>
> **—Garry Shandling**

• • •

The Siamese Twins Joke

Why did the Siamese twins move from California to London?

So the other one could drive.

•

A fighter was in the ring with Siamese twins.

After the bout he returned home and his wife asked, "Did you win?"

He answered, "Yes and no."

• • •

The Snail Joke

A snail bought a particularly impressive race car and decided to enter the 24 Hours of Le Mans. To give the car a distinctive look, the snail had a big letter S painted on the hood, sides and trunk before the big race. When the race began, the snail's car immediately took the lead, prompting one of the excited French spectators to cheer, "Just look at that S car go!"

•

A sloth was wandering through the brush one day when he was attacked by a vicious gang of snails who left him beaten and bloodied. When the sloth recovered, he made his way to the police station to report the attack. Asked to describe the assailants, he responded, "It all happened so fast, I couldn't catch what they looked like."

The Soldier Joke

A general noticed one of his soldiers behaving a bit out of the ordinary. The soldier would pick up any piece of paper put in front of him, look at it disdainfully and say, "That's not it" and put it down again.

At one point, the general arranged to have the soldier psychologically tested. The psychologist concluded that the soldier was mentally unfit for service, and wrote out his military discharge. The soldier picked it up, smiled and said: "That's it."

• • •

The Sportsman's Joke

A guy is eating a bald eagle and gets caught by the game warden. He's brought to trial for killing an endangered species. The judge says, "Are you aware that eating a bald eagle is a federal offense?"

The guy answers, "Yes, but I have an explanation... I got lost in the woods and didn't have anything to eat for two weeks. I saw this bald eagle swooping down for fish at the lake. I figured I might be able to steal some fish as the eagle grabbed them. Unfortunately, when I went to grab for the fish, my fist hit the eagle in the head and killed 'im. I reckoned that, since the eagle was dead, I might as well eat it since it would be a waste to just let it rot."

After a brief recess, the judge comes back with his ruling. "Due to the extreme conditions you endured, added to the fact that the bald eagle's death was accidental rather than intentional, I find you not guilty."

As an aside, the judge asks the guy, "By the way, what does a bald eagle taste like?"

The guy responds, "The best way to describe it is a cross between a spotted owl and a condor."

• • •

The Super Bowl Joke

A guy desperately wants to go to Super Bowl XXX, so he seeks out a scalper- but is only able to get one ticket. He pays top dollar for a seat in the nose-bleed section, the second to last row of the upper deck.

As the game begins, the guy's watching through his binoculars. He notices that there's an empty seat in the very first row, right on the fifty yard line. As the second quarter is about to end, he looks down and sees that the fifty yard line seat is still empty. At half-time, he makes his way down to the empty seat and asks the guy who's sitting in the next seat. "Is this taken?"

The guy replies, "No."

"Would you mind if I sit here?"

The other guy says, "Not at all. Go right ahead."

"I wonder why someone with a front row, fifty yard line seat wouldn't show up at the Super Bowl," says the first guy.

The second guy says, "Actually, my wife and I have come to every Super Bowl since 1967, but she passed away."

"Oh, gee, I'm sorry to hear that," says the first guy. "But couldn't you get a friend or relative to come to the game?"

"I tried to, but they're all at the funeral."

———— • ————

You should always go to other people's funerals; otherwise they won't come to yours.

—Yogi Berra

• • •

The Tennis Joke

A cat is watching a tennis match. Another cat strolls by and says, "Why are you watching that? Cats don't like tennis."

"I know...but my father's in the racket."

• • •

The Three Little Pigs Joke

Three Little Pigs went out to dinner one evening. When the waiter asked what they'd like to drink, the first little piggy said, "I would like a Pepsi."

"I would like a Sprite," said the second little piggy.

"I want beer – a big, big beer," said the third little piggy.

The drinks were brought out and the waiter took the pigs' orders for dinner.

"I want a T-bone steak," said the first piggy.

"I would like the chicken salad," said the second piggy.

"I want another beer- a big, big beer," said the third little piggy.

A while after the meals had been brought out, the waiter asked the three little pigs if they'd like any dessert.

"I want some apple pie," said the first piggy.

"I want an ice cream sundae," said the second piggy.

"I want another beer – a big, big beer," said the third little piggy."

"Excuse me for asking," said the waiter to the third little piggy, "but how come you've only ordered beer all evening?"

"Because," answered the third little piggy, "somebody has to go wee, wee, wee all the way home!"

• • •

The (World's Cleanest) Traveling Salesman Joke...

Tom went to Chicago to see his old buddy, Steve, who still ran the little corner grocery store that his father started a half-century ago.

Stepping into the store, Tom shook hands with his friend and they brought each other up to date. At one point, Tom became distracted as he saw that the shelves of the store were all filled with soap. As Tom was shown around the place, he couldn't help but notice that the stockroom was filled with soap and, out back, there was a fifty foot storage trailer filled with soap.

"Gee, pal," said Tom, shaking his head. "You sure do sell a lot of soap here!"

"Nah, not really," replied Steve. "But the guy who sold it to me...brother, could he sell soap!"

• • •

The Turtle Joke

Two turtles go fishing and pack a cooler with sandwiches and a six-pack. After five days of walking, they find a great spot at the lake, but they've forgotten the bottle opener. One turtle says to the other, "Why don't you go back and get the opener?"

The other turtle says, "No way. You'll eat all the food while I'm gone."

The first turtle says, "I promise I won't. Just hurry."

The second turtle leaves. Nine days later there's no sign of him. Finally, the first turtle opens up one of the sandwiches. The second turtle pops out from behind a rock and hollers, "I knew it! Now I'm not going!"

The Twins Joke

"Oh, Mrs. Owens," gushed the woman's teenaged babysitter visiting her in the maternity ward. "I can hardly believe it- triplets- how wonderful!"

"Yes it is Sally," replied the proud mother. "And did you know that triplets only happen once every 4,657,842 times?"

"4,657,842 times?" Sally gasped with amazement. "When did you ever find time to clean the house?"

• • •

The Ugly Joke

A wealthy man had a daughter who was rather homely, to say the least. In a desperate attempt to marry her off, the tycoon found an enterprising, available young gentleman by the name of William Randolph Hearst. He invited the fellow to dinner and, with the promise of a huge financial windfall, suggested Mr. Hearst wink at the girl during the meal. Unfortunately, once he saw her, no amount of money would have coaxed Hearst to bat his lashes, which just goes to show you: You can lead a Hearst to daughter, but you can't make him wink.

The Usher Joke

A husband bought front row tickets for he and his wife to see *Spamalot* on Broadway. When they arrived at the theatre, the husband had to use the men's room. Meanwhile, his wife meandered down to the front row only to find a man sprawled out on their seats.

"Excuse me, sir," said the wife timidly, "but I think these are our seats."

"Aaaaaaaaaaaggggghhhhh," gurgled the man.

The wife scampered up the steps to the back of the theatre where she met her husband, who was on his way back from the men's room. She told him what had happened and he immediately went down to the seats to confront the man himself.

"Excuse me, buddy, but I paid top dollar for these seats. You'll have to leave," demanded the husband.

The man remained prostrate on the seats and again responded, "Aaaaaaaaaaaggggghhhhh!"

At this point, the husband decided to complain to an usher who apologized for the inconvenience and promised to take care of the problem. The usher went down to the seats, approached the man and said, "Excuse me, sir. What's your name?"

"Geee-oooo-rrrr-ggg-e."

"Okay, George- where do you come from?"

"The baaaaaallllcccony!"

A guy sitting in the back of the theater motions to the usher. He whispers, "This is a mystery. A mystery must be seen close up. Get me a better seat and I'll take care of you."

The usher escorts him to a second row seat and the guy gives him a quarter. The usher leans over and whispers, "The wife did it."

———— • ————

**My uncle was thrown out of a mime show for having a seizure.
They thought he was heckling.**

—Jeff Shaw

• • •

The Waiter Joke

An old fellow orders a bowl of soup at a restaurant. The waiter brings him the soup and starts to walk away. The old guy beckons to the waiter and says, "Taste this soup."

"Is it too hot?" the waiter asks.

The old man shakes his head. "Taste it."

The waiter asks, "Is it too cold?"

"Taste it," the senior responds.

"Is it too spicy?" the waiter asks.

"I said, taste the soup."

Now the waiter is totally exasperated. "Okay, okay, I'll taste it... Where's the spoon?"

"Ah-ha!" says the old man gleefully.

A waiter dies suddenly and his widow is so distraught she seeks out a medium who assures her that she can speak to her husband. At the appointed time, the widow goes to a séance, presses her hands on the table and calls out, "Seymour, Seymour, speak to me!"

There's a terrible shriek and scary noises followed by a faint voice which cries out, "Sorry, it's not my table!"

• • •

The Waitress Joke

A man and a woman were at a fancy restaurant. They had placed their orders, but as the waitress was returning to bring their drinks, she noticed the man's head disappear under the tablecloth.

"Pardon me, ma'am, but I think your husband just slid under the table."

The woman calmly looked up at her and replied firmly, "No, my date just slid under the table- my husband just walked in the door."

•

If you ordered pasta and antipasta, would you still have an appetite?

The Widow Joke

Fenwick the farmhand suffers a fatal heart attack while on the job. The other farmers are trying to figure out a gentle way to break the news to his wife. None of them knows Mrs. Fenwick, so they elect the local sheriff to inform her since they assume he's had to do that sort of thing before. The sheriff rings the Fenwicks' doorbell. When a woman answers the door, he asks, "Are you the widow Fenwick?"

She responds, "No, I'm Mrs. Fenwick."

The sheriff says, "Not anymore."

• • •

The World War II Joke

During World War II, an Englishman, an Irishman and a former American college jock were captured in German territory and sentenced to death by a firing squad. The Englishman said to his comrades "I say chaps, it seems that we're up against the wall as it were. Our only chance is to create a diversion just before they shoot, and in the confusion, we'll escape."

The next morning at dawn, the three were marched outside the prison and the firing squad took its position. The officer raised his sword and commanded, "Ready, Aim..." and with that the Englishman yelled "Air raid!" As all the soldiers scrambled for cover, he made it over the wall.

The Nazi officer decided to look for him later and continued with the execution. He lined the two remaining prisoners up, raised his sword and said "Ready, Aim..." and just then the Irishman yelled "Earthquake!" Once again, the German troops scattered, affording him his chance to escape.

The disgusted officer formed up his firing squad for the one remaining prisoner, once again raised his sword and say "Ready, Aim..." Just then, the former college jock screamed at the top of his lungs "Fire!"

———— • ————

I'm desperately trying to figure out why kamikaze pilots wore helmets.

—Dave Edison

• • •

The World's Worst Joke

Y*ou know it. You've heard it. You may have told it- That extremely long-winded yarn with the pointless punch line, otherwise known as the shaggy dog joke. It's been around since way back when. When is that, you ask? Well, no one knows for sure but our dogged research has dug up what we believe to be the original shaggy dog story. Here goes...*

A wealthy English gentleman had his butler place full-page ads in newspapers all over the world, hoping to find his long lost, shaggy sheepdog. The finder's reward was a guarantee of a lifetime of luxury according to the dog-owner's plea. One morning over breakfast, a New York City fellow was reading the Times when he came across the advertisement. He didn't think much of it but later that day while strolling through Central Park, the fellow saw a stray sheepdog and recalled that it seemed to fit the description in the newspaper ad. The man left the park to buy a leash, returned and rounded up the pooch. The fellow bought a plane ticket for himself and the dog. They flew to London's Heathrow Airport and then hired a limo to escort them to the address cited in the advertisement. Once they arrived, the fellow rang the doorbell and the butler answered. He looked down at the dog and then said to the fellow, "Ah, yes. We're looking for a shaggy dog, but not so shaggy as **that**, sir!"

———— • ————

I have a dog that's half pit bull, half poodle. Not much of a guard dog, but a vicious gossip.

—Craig Shoemaker

• • •

The X Joke

A couple of ballplayers are at a sports memorabilia show. One says to the other, "My X is worth five hundred bucks."

The other says, "That's nothing. My ex is worth ten grand a month."

• • •

The Yodeling Joke

Knock Knock.

Who's there?

Little old lady.

Little old lady who?

I didn't know you could yodel.

The Z Joke

The jokes in this book have been presented in alphabetical order. But there'll be no embarrassed "zebra" joke here. Nor will there be the Mr. Lion at the z as in "zoo" joke. Instead, we invite you to send in your own z as in "zany" joke for possible inclusion in a future Bathroom Library funny book.

Please write to:

Life of the Potty
Red-Letter Press
P.O. Box 393
Saddle River, NJ 07458

— or —

e-mail us at:
info@Red-LetterPress.com